# 101 Great Recipes:
# A Cook Book

By

**CHEF JOHN DYE**

Order this book online at www.trafford.com
or email orders@trafford.com

Most Trafford titles are also available at major online book retailers.

Print information available on the last page.

ISBN: 978-1-4907-6862-5 (sc)
ISBN: 978-1-4907-6863-2 (hc)
ISBN: 978-1-4907-6864-9 (e)

Library of Congress Control Number: 2016900317

Because of the dynamic nature of the Internet, any web addresses or links contained in
this book may have changed since publication and may no longer be valid. The views
expressed in this work are solely those of the author and do not necessarily reflect the
views of the publisher, and the publisher hereby disclaims any responsibility for them.

Any people depicted in stock imagery provided by Thinkstock are models,
and such images are being used for illustrative purposes only.
Certain stock imagery © Thinkstock.

*Trafford rev. 02/08/2016*

 www.trafford.com
North America & international
toll-free: 1 888 232 4444 (USA & Canada)
fax: 812 355 4082

# TABLE OF CONTENTS

1.  Beef Chunks and Gravy over Rice
2.  Beef Chunks and Gravy over potatoes
3.  Beef Chunks in Beef Rice
4.  Beef Stew
5.  Beef Roast and Forked Potatoes
6.  Beef Ribs and Gravy over Rice
7.  Beef Ribs and Gravy over Forked Potatoes
8.  Oven Steak, Baked Potatoes and Green Beans
9.  Oven Steak, Forked Potatoes and Greens
10. Oven Steak and Steak Fries
11. Steak Fajitas
12. Dirty Rice with Hamburger
13. Hamburger Patties in Beefy Mushroom Gravy and Forked Potatoes
14. Bacon Cheeseburger Sandwich and Fries
15. Sloppy Joe Sandwich and Chips
16. Awesome Lasagna
17. Awesome Spaghetti
18. Awesome Chili
19. Chili and Spaghetti Mac Left-Over

1. Jambalaya with Chicken, Ham and Polish Sausage
2. Grilled Chicken Breast, Forked Potatoes and Green Beans
3. Baked Chicken Breast, Forked Potatoes and Greens
4. Baked Barbeque Chicken, Forked Potatoes and Green Beans
5. Chicken and Dressing
6. Roasted Chicken, Corn and Greens
7. Chicken Chunks and Broccoli Cheddar Rice Casserole
8. Cheesy Chicken Enchiladas
9. Fried Chicken and Smothered Potatoes
10. Fried Chicken Wing Sections in Favorite Hot Sauce
11. Fried Chicken Wing Sections in Favorite Barbeque Sauce
12. Fried Chicken Wing Sections in Jamaican Jerk Sauce
13. Fried Chicken Strips and Fries
14. Fried Chicken Breast Sandwich and Fries
15. Grilled Chicken Breast Sandwich and fries
16. Chicken Fajitas
17. Chicken, Beef and Polish Sausage Boil
18. Whole Fried Chicken Wings and Spaghetti
19. Chicken Stew Sauce over Rice

1. Pork Stew Sauce over Rice
2. Pulled Pork Sandwich and Chips
3. Fried Pork Chops and Spaghetti
4. Fried Pork Chops, Smothered Potatoes and Corn on the Cob
5. Fried Pork Chops Smothered in Gravy, Forked Potatoes and Biscuits
6. Fried Pork Chop Sandwich and Forked Potatoes
7. Baked Pork Chops, Forked Potatoes and Green Beans
8. Fried Pork Steak, Forked Potatoes and Corn on the Cob
9. Fried Pork Steaks Smothered in Gravy, Forked Potatoes and Biscuits
10. Baked Barbeque Pork Steak, Forked Potatoes and Green Beans
11. Fried Pork Rib-lets and Forked Potatoes
12. Fried Pork Rib-lets in Salsa over Rice
13. Oven Pork Barbeque Ribs, Macaroni & Cheese and Greens
14. Oven Country Barbeque Ribs, Macaroni & Cheese and Green Beans
15. Grilled Pork Ribs, Macaroni & Cheese and Green Beans
16. Smothered Potatoes and Polish Sausage
17. Smothered Cabbage and Polish Sausage
18. Fried Polish Sausage Sandwich and Fries
19. Fried Brat Sandwich and Forked Potatoes
20. Grilled Brats and Macaroni & Cheese
21. Baked Ham, Macaroni & Cheese and Greens
22. Fried Ham Sandwich and Chips
23. Fried Ham, Cheesy Eggs and Toast

24. Fried Diced Ham in Cheesy Eggs, O'Brien Potatoes and Toast
25. Fried Sausage, Ham, Bacon, Cheesy Eggs and Toast
26. Fried Crumbled Sausage in Rice
27. Fried Crumbled Italian Sausage and Rice in Stuffed Peppers
28. Tender Neck-bones and Forked Potatoes

1. Beef Stew
2. Chicken, Beef and Polish Sausage Boil
3. Chicken Stew Sauce over Rice
4. Pork Stew Sauce over Rice
5. Ham and Great Northern Beans
6. Ham and Pinto Beans
7. Bacon and Pinto Beans
8. Awesome Chili
9. Chili and Spaghetti Mac Left Over

# *"INTRODUCTION"*

Welcome, the first step in cooking good food is to go in the kitchen and get started right away.

Please don't hesitate, make some dish water; so you can clean while you prepare and cook the food. This saves time and a clean kitchen is half the battle.

Always season food to taste using seasoning salt, black pepper, onions, red and green peppers. This will give your food a good flavor, trust me. You will thank me later.

By Chef John Dye

# "Beef Chunks and Gravy over Potatoes"

<u>Makes 8 servings</u>

3 lbs. – beef stew meat

1 small onion sliced

1 small green bell pepper sliced

1 small red bell pepper sliced

1 tsp. season salt

1 tsp. black pepper

1 beef stew seasoning packet with 1 cup of water

1 brown gravy packet with 1 cup of water

8 potatoes – use forked potato recipe on page 91

1.  Lightly brown meat in skillet then sprinkle seasoning salt and black pepper on meat first. Place browned meat in roast pan or 9x13 cake pan then pour 1 cup of beef stew seasoning mix and 1 cup of brown gravy mix over meat.
2.  Cover with lid or aluminum foil and bake 30 minutes.
3.  Then uncover to add onions, green and red bell peppers. Cover and continue baking 15 minutes.
4.  Stir gravy to make sure everything is thoroughly mixed.
5.  30 minutes before meat is done. Cook potatoes according to page 91.

Put meat and potatoes on plates then pour gravy over potatoes and serve.

# "Beef Chunks and Gravy over Rice"

<u>Makes 8 servings</u>

3 lbs. - beef stew meat

1 small onion sliced

1 small green bell pepper sliced

1 small red bell pepper sliced

1 tsp. season salt

1 tsp. black pepper

1 beef stew seasoning packet with 1 cup of water

1 brown gravy packet with 1 cup of water

Rice – use Rice recipe on page 92 or Boil-a-bag rice in 10 minutes

1. Lightly brown meat in skillet then sprinkle seasoning salt and black pepper on meat first. Place browned meat in roast pan or 9x13 cake pan then pour 1 cup of beef stew seasoning mix and 1 cup of brown gravy mix over meat.
2. Cover with lid or aluminum foil and bake 30 minutes.
3. Then uncover to add onions, green and red bell peppers. Cover and continue baking 15 minutes.
4. Stir gravy to make sure everything is thoroughly mixed.
5. 10 minutes before meat is done. Cook rice according to page 92.

Put meat and rice on plates then pour gravy over rice and serve.

# "Beef Chunks in Beef Rice"

<u>Makes 8 servings</u>

3 lbs. - beef stew meat

1 small onion sliced

1 small green bell pepper sliced

1 small red bell pepper sliced

1 tsp. season salt

1 tsp. black pepper

2 small boxes of Rice a Roni

5 cups of water

1. Lightly brown meat in skillet then sprinkle seasoning salt and black pepper on meat first, also add onions, green and red bell peppers. Lightly brown rice & vermicelli with butter in another skillet. Place browned meat, beef seasoning packets, rice and vermicelli in 5 quart pot with 5 cups of water then stir.
2. Cover and cook on low 30 minutes.
3. Stir to make sure everything is thoroughly mixed.

Put beef rice in bowls and serve.

# "Beef Stew"

3 lbs. - beef stew meat

1 small onion sliced

1 small green bell pepper sliced

1 small red bell pepper sliced

1 tsp. season salt

1 tsp. black pepper

1 beef stew seasoning packet with 1 cup of water

3 cans mixed vegetables

1 small can of tomato paste and 1 8oz can of tomato sauce

2 cups of water

1. Lightly brown meat in skillet then sprinkle seasoning salt and black pepper on meat first. Place browned meat in 5 quart pot then pour 1 cup of beef stew seasoning mix over meat. Add 3 cans of mixed vegetables, tomato sauce, tomato paste and 2 cups of water.
2. Cover and cook 15 minutes.
3. Then uncover to add onions, green and red bell peppers. Cover and continue cooking on low 15 minutes.
4. Stir to make sure everything is thoroughly mixed.

Put beef stew in bowls and serve.

# "Beef Roast and Forked Potatoes"

<u>Makes 8 servings</u>

3 lbs. - beef roast

1 small onion sliced

1 small green bell pepper sliced

1 small red bell pepper sliced

1 tsp. season salt

1 tsp. black pepper

1 beef stew seasoning packet with 1 cup of water

1 brown gravy packet with 1 cup of water

8 potatoes – use forked potato recipe on page 91

1. Place roast in roast pan or 9x13 cake pan then sprinkle seasoning salt and black pepper on meat first, also pour 1 cup of beef stew seasoning mix and 1 cup of brown gravy mix over meat.
2. Cover with lid or aluminum foil and bake 1 hour.
3. Then uncover to add onions, green and red bell peppers. Cover and continue baking 1 hour.
4. Stir gravy to make sure everything is thoroughly mixed.
5. 30 minutes before meat is done. Cook potatoes according to page 91.

Put meat and potatoes on plates then pour gravy over potatoes and serve.

# "Beef Ribs and Gravy over Rice"

<u>Makes 8 servings</u>

1 slab of beef ribs

1 small onion sliced

1 small green bell pepper sliced

1 small red bell pepper sliced

1 tsp. season salt

1 tsp. black pepper

1 beef stew seasoning packet with 1 cup of water

1 brown gravy packet with 1 cup of water

Rice – use Rice recipe on page 92 or Boil-a-bag rice in 10 minutes

1. Cut slab in 1/3 then put in 5 quart pot and boil 30 minutes. Place slab of beef ribs in roast pan or 9x13 cake pan then sprinkle seasoning salt and black pepper on meat first, also pour 1 cup of beef stew seasoning mix and 1 cup of brown gravy mix over meat.
2. Cover with lid or aluminum foil and bake 30 minutes.
3. Then uncover to add onions, green and red bell peppers. Cover and continue baking 30 minutes.
4. Stir gravy to make sure everything is thoroughly mixed.
5. 10 minutes before meat is done. Cook rice according to page 92.

Put meat and rice on plates then pour gravy over rice and serve.

# "Beef Ribs and Gravy over Forked Potatoes"

<u>Makes 8 servings</u>

1 slab of beef ribs

1 small onion sliced

1 small green bell pepper sliced

1 small red bell pepper sliced

1 tsp. season salt

1 tsp. black pepper

1 beef stew seasoning packet with 1 cup of water

1 brown gravy packet with 1 cup of water

8 potatoes – use forked potato recipe on page 91

1. Cut slab in 1/3 then put in 5 quart pot and boil 30 minutes. Place slab of beef ribs in roast pan or 9x13 cake pan then sprinkle seasoning salt and black pepper on meat first, also pour 1 cup of beef stew seasoning mix and 1 cup of brown gravy mix over meat.
2. Cover with lid or aluminum foil and bake 30 minutes.
3. Then uncover to add onions, green and red bell peppers. Cover and continue baking 30 minutes.
4. Stir gravy to make sure everything is thoroughly mixed.
5. 30 minutes before meat is done. Cook potatoes according to page 91.

Put meat and potatoes on plates then pour gravy over potatoes and serve.

# "Oven Steak, Bake Potatoes and Green Beans"

<u>Makes 2 servings</u>

2 porter house steaks (or your favorite steaks)

1 small onion sliced

1 small green bell pepper sliced

1 small red bell pepper sliced

1 tsp. season salt

1 tsp. black pepper

1 beef stew seasoning packet with 1 cup of water

2 15oz can of glory green beans or page 93

2 large Idaho potatoes (poke then bake in aluminum foil 2 hours)

1. Poke potatoes then wrap in aluminum foil and bake 2 hours, but put in oven, 1hour before you start meat.
2. Lightly brown meat in skillet then sprinkle seasoning salt and black pepper on meat first. Place browned meat in roast pan or 9x13 cake pan then pour 1 cup of beef stew seasoning mix over meat.
3. Cover with lid or aluminum foil and bake 30 minutes.
4. Then uncover to add onions, green and red bell peppers. Cover and continue baking 15 minutes.
5. Stir gravy to make sure everything is thoroughly mixed.
6. 30 minutes before meat is done. Cook green beans according to page 93.

Put meat, green beans and potatoes on plates then serve with butter and sour cream.

# "Oven Steak, Forked Potatoes and Greens"

<u>Makes 2 servings</u>

2 porter house steaks (or your favorite steaks)

1 small onion sliced

1 small green bell pepper sliced

1 small red bell pepper sliced

1 tsp. season salt

1 tsp. black pepper

1 beef stew seasoning packet with 1 cup of water

2 15oz cans of glory greens - recipe on page 95

1 15oz can of cut spinach

8 potatoes – use forked potato recipe on page 91

1. Lightly brown meat in skillet then sprinkle seasoning salt and black pepper on meat first. Place browned meat in roast pan or 9x13 cake pan then pour 1 cup of beef stew seasoning mix over meat.
2. Cover with lid or aluminum foil and bake 30 minutes.
3. Then uncover to add onions, green and red bell peppers. Cover and continue baking 15 minutes.
4. Stir gravy to make sure everything is thoroughly mixed.
5. 30 minutes before meat is done. Cook potatoes according to page 91 and make greens page 95.

Put meat, greens and potatoes on plates then pour gravy over potatoes and serve.

# "Oven Steak and Steak Fries"

<u>Makes 2 servings</u>

2 porter house steaks (or your favorite steaks)

1 small onion sliced

1 small green bell pepper sliced

1 small red bell pepper sliced

1 tsp. season salt

1 tsp. black pepper

1 beef stew seasoning packet with 1 cup of water

1 bag of steak fries

1. Lightly brown meat in skillet then sprinkle seasoning salt and black pepper on meat first. Place browned meat in roast pan or 9x13 cake pan then pour 1 cup of beef stew seasoning mix over meat.
2. Cover with lid or aluminum foil and bake 30 minutes
3. Then uncover to add onions, green and red bell peppers. Cover and continue baking 15 minutes.
4. Stir gravy to make sure everything is thoroughly mixed.
5. 30 minutes before meat is done. Cook steak fries according to package.

Put meat and fries on plates then serve.

# *"Steak Fajitas"*

<u>Makes 8 servings</u>

3 lbs. – sirloin steak

1 small onion sliced

1 small green bell pepper sliced

1 small red bell pepper sliced

1 tsp. season salt

1 tsp. black pepper

2 fajita seasoning packet with 2 cups of water

1 8oz package of blended cheeses

1 8oz can of diced tomatoes and 1 tub of sour cream

10 soft shell tortillas

1. Lightly brown (cut up) meat in skillet then sprinkle seasoning salt and black pepper on meat first.
2. Cover and cook 15 minutes.
3. Then uncover to add fajita seasoning with 2 cups of water, onions, green and red bell peppers to meat.
4. Cover and continue cooking on low 15 minutes.
5. Stir to make sure everything is thoroughly mixed.
6. 15 minutes before meat is done. Warm tortilla shells according package.

Put meat mixture & any other toppings in soft shell tortillas then place on plates with chips & salsa. Serve with your favorite drink.

# "Dirty Rice with Hamburger"

<u>Makes 8 servings</u>

3 lbs. - hamburger

1 small onion sliced

1 small green bell pepper sliced

1 small red bell pepper sliced

1 tsp. season salt

1 tsp. black pepper

2 small boxes of Dirty Rice

5 cups of water

1. Lightly brown meat in skillet then sprinkle seasoning salt and black pepper on meat first, also add onions, green and red bell peppers.
2. Place browned meat and dirty rice mix in 5 quart pot with 5 cups of water then stir.
3. Cover and cook on low 25 minutes.
4. Stir to make sure everything is thoroughly mixed.

Put dirty rice in bowls and serve.

# "Hamburger Patties in Beefy Mushroom Gravy and Forked Potatoes"

<u>Makes 8 servings</u>

3 lbs. - hamburger

1 small onion sliced

1 small green bell pepper sliced

1 small red bell pepper sliced

1 tsp. season salt

1 tsp. black pepper

1 beef stew seasoning packet with 1 cup of water

1 brown gravy packet with 1 cup of water

8 potatoes – use forked potato recipe on page 91

1. Brown 8 hamburger patties in skillet then sprinkle seasoning salt and black pepper on meat first. Place browned patties and onions, green and red bell peppers in roast pan or 9x13 cake pan then pour 1 cup of beef stew seasoning mix and 1 cup of brown gravy mix over meat.
2. Cover with lid or aluminum foil and bake 30 minutes.
3. Stir gravy to make sure everything is thoroughly mixed.
4. 30 minutes before meat is done. Cook potatoes according to page 91.

Put meat and potatoes on plates then pour gravy over potatoes and serve.

# "Bacon Cheeseburger Sandwich and Fries"

<u>Makes 8 servings</u>

3 lbs. - hamburger

1 small onion sliced

1 tsp. season salt

1 tsp. black pepper

1 bottle of ketchup

1 bottle of mustard

1 tomato and 1 head of lettuce

1 bag of your favorite fries

1. Brown 8 hamburger patties in skillet then sprinkle seasoning salt and black pepper on meat first. When meat is done, put cheese on top of patties for 1 minute.
2. Place cheese patties on buns with ketchup, mustard, onions, tomatoes and lettuce.
3. 30 minutes before meat is done. Cook fries according to package.

Put sandwiches and fries on plates then serve.

# "Sloppy Joe Sandwich and Chips"

<u>Makes 8 servings</u>

3 lbs. - hamburger

1 small onion sliced

1 small green bell pepper sliced

1 small red bell pepper sliced

1 tsp. season salt

1 tsp. black pepper

2 cans of manwich sloppy joe sauce

1 bag of favorite chips

1. Brown meat in skillet then sprinkle seasoning salt and black pepper on meat first, also add onions, green and red bell peppers then pour 2 cans of manwich sloppy joe mixture over meat.
2. Cover and cook on low 25 minutes.
3. Place browned meat mixture on buns.

Put sandwiches and favorite chips on plates then serve.

# *"Awesome Lasagna"*

<u>Makes 8 servings</u>

3 lbs. - hamburger

1 small onion sliced

1 small green bell pepper sliced

1 small red bell pepper sliced

1 tsp. season salt and 1 tsp. black pepper

2 tubs of ricotta cheese

1 package of shredded mozzarella cheese & 1 blended cheese

1 jar of favorite spaghetti sauce

1 can of tomato sauce

1 package of lasagna noodles

1. Boil lasagna noodles in 5 quart pot 10 minutes and drain.
2. Mix mozzarella and blended cheeses together.
3. Brown meat in skillet then sprinkle seasoning salt and black pepper on meat first, also add onions, green and red bell peppers then pour spaghetti sauce and tomato sauce over meat.
4. Cover and cook 15 minutes.
5. Layer browned meat mixture, ricotta cheese and cheese mixture over noodles. The top should be noodles remaining meat mixture and cheese mixture in 9x13 cake pan.
6. Cover with aluminum foil and bake 45 minutes then uncover and continue baking 15 minutes.

Put lasagna on plates and serve.

# *"Awesome Spaghetti"*

<u>Makes 8 servings</u>

3 lbs. - hamburger

1 small onion sliced

1 small green bell pepper sliced

1 small red bell pepper sliced

1 tsp. season salt

1 tsp. black pepper

1 jar of favorite spaghetti sauce

1 can of tomato juice

1 package of spaghetti elbow noodles

1. Boil spaghetti noodles in 5 quart pot 10 minutes and drain.
2. Brown meat in skillet then sprinkle seasoning salt and black pepper on meat first, also add onions, green and red bell peppers then pour spaghetti sauce over meat.
3. Cover and cook 15 minutes.
4. Place browned meat mixture over spaghetti noodles and stir thoroughly.
5. Cover and cook on low 25 minutes.

Put spaghetti on plates and serve.

# "Awesome Chili"

<u>Makes 8 servings</u>

3 lbs. - hamburger

1 small onion sliced

1 small green bell pepper sliced

1 small red bell pepper sliced

1 tsp. season salt

1 tsp. black pepper

1 chili seasoning packet with 1 cup of water

1 small can of tomato paste

1 can of diced tomatoes

2 cans of Hormel chili with beans and 2 cans of chili beans

1. Brown meat in skillet then sprinkle seasoning salt and black pepper on meat first, also add onions, green and red bell peppers then pour 1 cup of chili seasoning mix over meat.
2. Cover and cook 15 minutes.
3. Put diced tomatoes, hormel chili with beans and chili beans in 5 quart pot.
4. Place browned meat mixture over bean mixture in 5 quart pot and stir thoroughly.
5. Cover and cook on low 25 minutes.

Put chili in bowls and serve.

# "Chili and Spaghetti Mac Left-Over"

<u>Makes 8 servings</u>

3 lbs. - Hamburger

1 small onion sliced

1 small green bell pepper sliced

1 small red bell pepper sliced

1 tsp. season salt

1 tsp. black pepper

1 jar of favorite spaghetti sauce

1 can of tomato juice

1 package of spaghetti elbow noodles

1 chili seasoning packet with 1 cup of water

1 small can of tomato paste

1 can of diced tomatoes

2 cans of Hormel chili with beans and 2 cans of chili beans

1. Put left over spaghetti and left over chili in 5 quart pot together and stir thoroughly.
2. Cover and cook on low 25 minutes.

Put chili-mac in bowls and serve.

# "Jambalaya with Chicken, Ham and Polish Sausage"

<u>Makes 8 servings</u>

1 lb. diced chicken, 1 lb. diced ham and 1 lb. diced polish sausage

1 small onion sliced

1 small green bell pepper sliced

1 small red bell pepper sliced

1 tsp. season salt

1 tsp. black pepper

2 small boxes of jambalaya

5 cups of water

1.  Lightly brown meat in skillet then sprinkle seasoning salt and black pepper on meat first, also add onions, green and red bell peppers. Place browned meat and jambalaya mix in 5 quart pot with 5 cups of water then stir.
2.  Cover and cook on low 30 minutes.
3.  Stir to make sure everything is thoroughly mixed.

Put jambalaya in bowls and serve.

# "Grilled Chicken Breast, Forked Potatoes and Green Beans"

<u>Makes 8 servings</u>

3 lbs. – chicken breast

1 small onion sliced

1 small green bell pepper sliced

1 small red bell pepper sliced

1 tsp. season salt

1 tsp. black pepper

2 15oz cans of glory green beans - recipe on page 93

8 potatoes – use forked potato recipe on page 91

1. Lightly brown meat on grill then sprinkle seasoning salt and black pepper on meat first.
2. 30 minutes before meat is done. Cook potatoes according to page 91 and make green beans page 93.

Put meat, green beans and potatoes on plates then serve.

# "Baked Chicken Breast, Forked Potatoes and Greens"

<u>Makes 8 servings</u>

3 lbs. – chicken breast

1 small onion sliced

1 small green bell pepper sliced

1 small red bell pepper sliced

1 tsp. season salt

1 tsp. black pepper

1 can of cream of chicken

2 15oz cans of glory greens - recipe on page 95

1 15oz can of cut spinach

8 potatoes – use forked potato recipe on page 91

1. Lightly brown meat in skillet then sprinkle seasoning salt and black pepper on meat first. Place browned meat in roast pan or 9x13 cake pan then pour 1 can of cream of chicken sauce over meat.
2. Cover with lid or aluminum foil and bake 15 minutes.
3. Then uncover to add onions, green and red bell peppers. Cover and continue baking 15 minutes.
4. Stir gravy to make sure everything is thoroughly mixed.
5. 30 minutes before meat is done. Cook potatoes according to page 91 and make greens page 95.

Put meat, greens and potatoes on plates then pour gravy over potatoes and serve.

# "Baked Barbeque Chicken, Forked Potatoes and Green Beans"

<u>Makes 8 servings</u>

3 lbs. – chicken breast

1 small onion sliced

1 small green bell pepper sliced

1 small red bell pepper sliced

1 tsp. season salt

1 tsp. black pepper

2 bottles of favorite barbeque sauce (Thick and spicy /the best)

2 15oz cans of glory green beans - recipe on page 93

8 potatoes – use forked potato recipe on page 91

1. Lightly brown meat in skillet then sprinkle seasoning salt and black pepper on meat first. Place browned meat in roast pan or 9x13 cake pan then pour barbeque sauce over meat.
2. Cover with lid or aluminum foil and bake 15 minutes.
3. Then uncover to add more barbeque sauce, onions, green and red bell peppers and continue baking uncovered 15 minutes.
4. 30 minutes before meat is done. Cook potatoes according to page 91 and make green beans page 93.

Put meat, green beans and potatoes on plates then serve.

# "Chicken and Dressing"

3 lbs. – chicken breast

1 small onion sliced

1 small green bell pepper sliced

1 cup of diced celery

1 tsp. season salt

1 tsp. black pepper

2 chicken gravy packets with 1 cup of water

1 box of chicken broth

1. Make a 9x13 pan of corn bread according to package. Let cool 15 minutes then crumble corn bread in roast pan or 9x13 cake pan and sprinkle in onion, green bell peppers and diced celery.
2. Boil chicken breast 15 minutes.
3. Lightly brown meat in skillet then sprinkle seasoning salt and black pepper on meat first, also shred meat. Place browned shredded meat in roast pan or 9x13 cake pan with corn bread crumbs then pour chicken broth and gravy sauce over meat until thoroughly saturated or moist. Add 2 eggs and stir.
4. Cover with lid or aluminum foil and bake 1 hour.

Put chicken dressing on plates and sprinkle a little franks red hot sauce over dressing then serve.

# "Roasted Chicken, Corn and Greens"

<u>Makes 8 servings</u>

3 lbs. – chicken or 1 whole chicken

1 small onion sliced

1 small green bell pepper sliced

1 small red bell pepper sliced

1 tsp. season salt

1 tsp. black pepper

2 15oz cans of glory greens - recipe on page 95

1 15oz can of cut spinach

2 8oz cans of corn

1. First rub vegetable oil all over chicken then sprinkle seasoning salt and black pepper on meat first.
2. Place chicken in clear baking bag with onions, green and red bell peppers then tie bag closed.
3. Bake 1 hour.
4. 30 minutes before chicken is done. Cook greens according to page 95 and make corn in sauce pan with butter.

Put meat, greens and corn on plates then serve.

# "Chicken Chunks and Broccoli Cheddar Rice Casserole"

<u>Makes 8 servings</u>

3 lbs. – chicken chunks or diced chicken

1 small onion sliced

1 small green bell pepper sliced

1 small red bell pepper sliced

1 tsp. season salt

1 tsp. black pepper

2 broccoli and cheddar rice packages with 2 cups of water

1 can of grand butter milk biscuits or page 104

1. Boil broccoli cheddar rice according to package in 5 quart pot 15 minutes then pour in roast pan or 9x13 cake pan.
2. Lightly brown meat in skillet then sprinkle seasoning salt and black pepper on meat first. Place browned meat in roast pan or 9x13 cake pan with broccoli cheddar rice and stir thoroughly then cover mixture with blended cheeses.
3. Cover with lid or aluminum foil and bake 25 minutes.
4. 10 minutes before meal is done. Cook biscuits according to page 104 with butter.

Put meal on plates with biscuits and serve.

# *"Cheesy Chicken Enchiladas"*

<u>Makes 8 servings</u>

3 lbs. – chicken breast

1 small onion sliced

1 small green bell pepper sliced

1 tsp. season salt

1 tsp. black pepper

2 8oz packages of blended cheese

2 fajita seasoning packets with 2 cup of water

1 15oz can of enchilada sauce

1 package of large burrito soft shells

1. Boil chicken breast 10 minutes in 5 quart pot.
2. Lightly brown meat in skillet then sprinkle seasoning salt and black pepper on meat first.
3. Cover and cook 10 minutes.
4. Then uncover shred meat and add fajita seasoning with 2 cups of water, onions, green and red bell peppers to meat.
5. Cover and continue cooking 10 minutes.
6. Stir to make sure everything is thoroughly mixed.
7. Wrap browned shredded meat in burrito shells and place in roast pan or 9x13 cake pan. Pour enchilada sauce over burrito shells then spread blended cheeses over sauce.
8. Cover with lid or aluminum foil and bake 25 minutes.

Put meal on plates and serve.

# "Fried Chicken and Smothered Potatoes"

3 lbs. – whole cut up chicken

1 small onion sliced

1 small green bell pepper sliced

1 small red bell pepper sliced

1 tsp. season salt

1 tsp. black pepper

8 potatoes – use smothered potato recipe on page 65

1. Place cut up chicken in 9x13 cake pan then sprinkle seasoning salt and black pepper on meat first, also take a plastic bag and put flour in it. Use a double bag method, so flour won't spill out of the bag.
2. Toss individual pieces of chicken in bag and shake until coated with flour. Pour vegetable oil in a skillet and heat oil until it pops a little. (Important) Place chicken in hot skillet.
3. Cover and fry chicken until golden brown on one side.
4. Then uncover and fry chicken until golden brown on the other side. (Only cook 4 pieces at a time)
5. 30 minutes before chicken is done. Cook potatoes according to page 65.

Put meat and potatoes on plates then serve.

# "Fried Chicken Wing Sections in Favorite Hot Sauce"

<u>Makes 8 servings</u>

3 lbs. – cut up chicken wings

1 small onion sliced

1 small green bell pepper sliced

1 small red bell pepper sliced

1 tsp. season salt

1 tsp. black pepper

1 bottle of your favorite hot sauce (Franks red hot /the best)

1 bag of your favorite fries

1. Cut chicken wings in half or sections.
2. Place cut up chicken in 9x13 cake pan then sprinkle seasoning salt and black pepper on meat first.
3. Pour vegetable oil in a skillet and heat oil until it pops a little. (Important) Place chicken in hot skillet.
4. Fry chicken uncovered until golden brown on both sides.
5. Place chicken in a metal or glass bowl then pour hot sauce over wings and toss until completely coated with sauce. (Only cook 6 pieces at a time)
6. 30 minutes before chicken is done. Cook fries according to package.

Put meat and fries on plates then serve.

# "Fried Chicken Wing Sections in Favorite Barbeque Sauce"

<u>Makes 8 servings</u>

3 lbs. – cut up chicken wings

1 small onion sliced

1 small green bell pepper sliced

1 small red bell pepper sliced

1 tsp. season salt

1 tsp. black pepper

1 bottle of your favorite barbeque sauce (Thick & spicy /the best)

1 bag of your favorite fries

1. Cut chicken wings in half or sections.
2. Place cut up chicken in 9x13 cake pan then sprinkle seasoning salt and black pepper on meat first.
3. Pour vegetable oil in a skillet and heat oil until it pops a little. (Important) Place chicken in hot skillet.
4. Fry chicken uncovered until golden brown on both sides.
5. Place chicken in a metal or glass bowl then pour barbeque sauce over wings and toss until completely coated with sauce. (Only cook 6 pieces at a time)
6. 30 minutes before chicken is done. Cook fries according to package.

Put meat and fries on plates then serve.

# "Fried Chicken Wing Sections in Jamaican Jerk Sauce"

<u>Makes 8 servings</u>

3 lbs. – cut up chicken wings

1 small onion sliced

1 small green bell pepper sliced

1 small red bell pepper sliced

1 tsp. season salt

1 tsp. black pepper

1 bottle of your favorite jerk sauce

1 bag of your favorite fries

1. Cut chicken wings in half or sections.
2. Place cut up chicken in 9x13 cake pan then sprinkle seasoning salt and black pepper on meat first.
3. Pour vegetable oil in a skillet and heat oil until it pops a little. (Important) Place chicken in hot skillet.
4. Fry chicken uncovered until golden brown on both sides.
5. Place chicken in a metal or glass bowl then pour jerk sauce over wings and toss until completely coated with sauce. (Only cook 6 pieces at a time)
6. 30 minutes before chicken is done. Cook fries according to package.

Put meat and fries on plates then serve.

# "Chicken Strips and Fries"

<u>Makes 8 servings</u>

3 lbs. – chicken breast

1 small onion sliced

1 small green bell pepper sliced

1 small red bell pepper sliced

1 tsp. season salt

1 tsp. black pepper

1 bag of your favorite fries

1. Cut chicken breast in half to make strips.
2. Place cut up chicken in 9x13 cake pan then sprinkle seasoning salt and black pepper on meat first, also take a plastic bag and put flour in it. Use a double bag method, so flour won't spill out of the bag.
3. Toss individual pieces of chicken in bag and shake until coated with flour. Pour vegetable oil in a skillet and heat oil until it pops a little. (Important) Place chicken in hot skillet.
4. Cover and fry chicken until golden brown on one side.
5. Then uncover and fry chicken until golden brown on the other side. (Only cook 4 pieces at a time)
6. 30 minutes before chicken is done. Cook fries according to package.

Put meat and fries on plates then serve.

# "Fried Chicken Breast Sandwich and Fries"

<u>Makes 8 servings</u>

3 lbs. – chicken breast

1 small onion sliced

1 small green bell pepper sliced

1 small red bell pepper sliced

1 tsp. season salt

1 tsp. black pepper

1 jar of mayonnaise

1 tomato and 1 head of lettuce

1 bag of your favorite fries

1. Place cut up chicken in 9x13 cake pan then sprinkle seasoning salt and black pepper on meat first also take a plastic bag and put flour in it. Use a double bag method, so flour won't spill out of the bag.
2. Toss individual pieces of chicken in bag and shake until coated with flour. Pour vegetable oil in a skillet and heat oil until it pops a little. (Important) Place chicken in hot skillet.
3. Cover and fry chicken until golden brown on one side.
4. Then uncover and fry chicken until golden brown on the other side. (Only cook 4 pieces at a time)
5. Place chicken breast on buns with mayonnaise, onions, tomatoes and lettuce.
6. 30 minutes before meat is done. Cook fries according to package.

Put sandwiches and fries on plates then serve.

# "Grilled Chicken Breast Sandwich and Fries"

<u>Makes 8 servings</u>

3 lbs. – chicken breast

1 small onion sliced

1 small green bell pepper sliced

1 small red bell pepper sliced

1 tsp. season salt

1 tsp. black pepper

1 bottle of mayonnaise

1 tomato and 1 head of lettuce

1 bag of your favorite fries

1. Place chicken in 9x13 cake pan then sprinkle seasoning salt and black pepper on meat first.
2. Heat grill. (Important) Place chicken on hot grill.
3. Grill chicken uncovered until brown on both sides.
4. Place chicken breast on buns with mayonnaise, onions, tomatoes and lettuce.
5. 30 minutes before meat is done. Cook fries according to package.

Put sandwiches and fries on plates then serve.

# "Chicken Fajitas"

<u>Makes 8 servings</u>

3 lbs. – chicken breast

1 small onion sliced

1 small green bell pepper sliced

1 tsp. season salt

1 tsp. black pepper

2 fajita seasoning packets with 2 cups of water

1 8oz packages of blended cheese

1 8oz can of diced tomatoes and 1 tub of sour cream

1 package of large burrito soft shells

1. Boil chicken breast 10 minutes in 5 quart pot.
2. Lightly brown meat in skillet then sprinkle seasoning salt and black pepper on meat first.
3. Cover and cook 10 minutes.
4. Then uncover shred meat and add fajita seasoning with 2 cups of water, onions, green and red bell peppers to meat.
5. Cover and continue cooking on low 10 minutes.
6. Stir to make sure everything is thoroughly mixed.
7. 15 minutes before meat is done. Warm tortilla shells according package.

Put meat mixture & any other toppings in soft shell tortillas then place on plates with chips & salsa. Serve with your favorite drink.

# "Chicken, Beef and Polish Sausage Boil"

<u>Makes 8 servings</u>

1 lb. diced chicken, 1 lb. diced beef and 1 lb. diced polish sausage

1 small onion sliced

1 small green bell pepper sliced

1 small red bell pepper sliced

1 tsp. season salt

1 tsp. black pepper

1 beef stew seasoning packet with 1 cup of water

3 cut up potatoes and 8 corn on the cob sections

1 15oz can of glory green beans

1 small can of tomato paste

2 cups of water

1. Lightly brown meat in separate skillets then sprinkle seasoning salt and black pepper on meat first. Place browned meats in 5 quart pot then pour 1 cup of beef stew seasoning mix over meat. Add 3 cut up potatoes, 8 corn on the cob sections, glory green beans, tomato paste and 2 cups of water.
2. Cover and cook 15 minutes.
3. Then uncover to add onions, green and red bell peppers. Cover and continue cooking on low 15 minutes.
4. Stir to make sure everything is thoroughly mixed.

Put stew in bowls and serve.

# "Whole Fried Chicken Wings and Spaghetti"

<u>Makes 8 servings</u>

3 lbs. – whole chicken wings

1 small onion sliced

1 small green bell pepper sliced

1 small red bell pepper sliced

1 tsp. season salt

1 tsp. black pepper

1 jar of favorite spaghetti sauce

1 can of tomato juice

1 package of spaghetti – use spaghetti recipe on page 28

1. Place cut up chicken in 9x13 cake pan then sprinkle seasoning salt and black pepper on meat first, also take a plastic bag and put flour in it. Use a double bag method, so flour won't spill out of the bag.
2. Toss individual pieces of chicken in bag and shake until coated with flour. Pour vegetable oil in a skillet and heat oil until it pops a little. (Important) Place chicken in hot skillet.
3. Cover and fry chicken until golden brown on one side.
4. Then uncover and fry chicken until golden brown on the other side. (Only cook 4 pieces at a time)
5. 30 minutes before chicken is done. Cook spaghetti according to page 28. (Elbow noodles are best)

Put meat and spaghetti on plates then serve.

# "Chicken Stew Sauce over Rice"

<u>Makes 8 servings</u>

3 lbs. – whole cut up chicken

1 small onion sliced

1 small green bell pepper sliced

1 small red bell pepper sliced

1 tsp. season salt

1 tsp. black pepper

2 cans mixed vegetables and 1 15oz can of glory green beans

1 small can of tomato paste and 1 8oz tomato sauce

1 cup of water

Rice – use Rice recipe on page 92 or Boil-a-bag rice in 10 minutes

1. Boil chicken 15 minutes in 5 quart pot then sprinkle seasoning salt and black pepper on meat first.
2. Uncover and de-bone meat. Place meat only in 5 quart pot then add 2 cans of mixed vegetables, glory green beans, tomato sauce, tomato paste, onions, green and red bell peppers and 1 cup of water.
3. Cover and cook 15 minutes.
4. Stir to make sure everything is thoroughly mixed.
5. 10 minutes before meal is done. Cook rice according to page 92

Put chicken stew sauce over rice on plates and serve.

# "Pork Stew Sauce over Rice"

<u>Makes 8 servings</u>

3 lbs. – cut up pork chops

1 small onion sliced

1 small green bell pepper sliced

1 small red bell pepper sliced

1 tsp. season salt

1 tsp. black pepper

1 beef stew seasoning packet with 1 cup of water

2 cans mixed vegetables and 1 15oz can of glory green beans

1 small can of tomato paste and 1 8oz tomato sauce

1 cup of water

Rice – use Rice recipe on page 92 or Boil-a-bag rice in 10 minutes

1. Boil cut up pork chops 15 minutes in 5 quart pot then sprinkle seasoning salt and black pepper on meat first.
2. Place meat only in 5 quart pot then pour1 cup of beef stew seasoning mix over meat. Add 2 cans of mixed vegetables, glory green beans, tomato sauce, tomato paste, onions, green and red bell peppers and 1 cup of water.
3. Cover and cook 15 minutes.
4. Stir to make sure everything is thoroughly mixed.
5. 10 minutes before meal is done. Cook rice according to page 92.

Put pork stew sauce over rice on plates and serve.

# *"Pulled Pork Sandwiches and Chips"*

<u>Makes 8 servings</u>

3 lbs. – shredded pork

1 small onion sliced

1 small green bell pepper sliced

1 small red bell pepper sliced

1 tsp. season salt

1 tsp. black pepper

2 bottles of favorite barbeque sauce (Thick and spicy /the best)

1 bag of favorite chips

1. Brown meat in skillet then sprinkle seasoning salt and black pepper on meat first, also add onions, green and red bell peppers then pour 2 bottles of barbeque sauce over meat.
2. Cover and cook on low for 25 minutes.
3. Place browned meat mixture on buns.

Put sandwiches and favorite chips on plates then serve.

# "Fried Pork Chops and Spaghetti"

<u>Makes 8 servings</u>

3 lbs. – pork chops

1 small onion sliced

1 small green bell pepper sliced

1 small red bell pepper sliced

1 tsp. season salt

1 tsp. black pepper

1 jar of favorite spaghetti sauce

1 can of tomato juice

1 package of spaghetti – use spaghetti recipe on page 28

1. Place pork chops in 9x13 cake pan then sprinkle seasoning salt and black pepper on meat first, also take a plastic bag and put flour in it. Use a double bag method, so flour won't spill out of the bag.
2. Toss individual pieces of meat in bag and shake until coated with flour. Pour vegetable oil in a skillet and heat oil until it pops a little. (Important) Place meat in hot skillet.
3. Cover and fry meat until golden brown on one side.
4. Then uncover and fry meat until golden brown on the other side. (Only cook 4 pieces at a time)
5. 30 minutes before meat is done. Cook spaghetti according to page 28. (Elbow noodles are best)

Put meat and spaghetti on plates then serve.

# "Fried Pork Chops, Smothered Potatoes and Corn on the Cob"

<u>Makes 8 servings</u>

3 lbs. – pork chops

1 small onion sliced

1 small green bell pepper sliced

1 small red bell pepper sliced

1 tsp. season salt

1 tsp. black pepper

8 potatoes – use smothered potato recipe on page 65

1. Place pork chops in 9x13 cake pan then sprinkle seasoning salt and black pepper on meat first, also take a plastic bag and put flour in it. Use a double bag method, so flour won't spill out of the bag.
2. Toss individual pieces of meat in bag and shake until coated with flour. Pour vegetable oil in a skillet and heat oil until it pops a little. (Important) Place meat in hot skillet.
3. Cover and fry meat until golden brown on one side.
4. Then uncover and fry meat until golden brown on the other side. (Only cook 4 pieces at a time)
5. 30 minutes before meat is done. Cook potatoes according to page 65 and boil corn on the cob 10 minutes.

Put meat, potatoes and corn on the cob on plates then serve.

# "Fried Pork Chops Smothered in gravy, Forked Potatoes and Biscuits"

<u>Makes 8 servings</u>

3 lbs. – pork chops

1 small onion sliced

1 small green bell pepper sliced

1 small red bell pepper sliced

1 tsp. season salt and 1 tsp. black pepper

2 brown gravy packets with 2 cups of water

1 can of grand butter milk biscuits - recipe on page 104

8 potatoes – use forked potato recipe on page 91

1. Place pork chops in 9x13 cake pan then sprinkle seasoning salt and black pepper on meat first, also take a plastic bag and put flour in it. Use a double bag method, so flour won't spill out of the bag.
2. Toss individual pieces of meat in bag and shake until coated with flour. Pour vegetable oil in a skillet and heat oil until it pops a little. (Important) Place meat in hot skillet.
3. Cover and fry meat until golden brown on one side.
4. Then uncover and fry meat until golden brown on the other side. (Only cook 4 pieces at a time) Drain grease from skillet then Place browned pork chops and onions, green and red bell peppers in skillet then pour 2 cups of brown gravy mix over meat. Cover and cook 15 minutes.
5. 30 minutes before meat is done. Cook potatoes according to page 91 and make biscuits page 104 with butter.

Put meat and potatoes on plates with biscuits then pour gravy over potatoes and serve.

# *"Fried Pork Chop Sandwich and Forked Potatoes"*

<u>Makes 8 servings</u>

3 lbs. – pork chops

1 small onion sliced

1 small green bell pepper sliced

1 small red bell pepper sliced

1 tsp. season salt

1 tsp. black pepper

8 potatoes – use forked potato recipe on page 91

1. Place pork chops in 9x13 cake pan then sprinkle seasoning salt and black pepper on meat first, also take a plastic bag and put flour in it. Use a double bag method, so flour won't spill out of the bag.
2. Toss individual pieces of meat in bag and shake until coated with flour. Pour vegetable oil in a skillet and heat oil until it pops a little. (Important) Place meat in hot skillet.
3. Cover and fry meat until golden brown on one side.
4. Then uncover and fry meat until golden brown on the other side. (Only cook 4 pieces at a time)
5. Place pork chops on buns with hot sauce.
6. 30 minutes before meat is done. Cook potatoes according to page 91.

Put sandwiches and potatoes on plates then serve.

# "Baked Pork Chops, Forked Potatoes and Green Beans"

<u>Makes 8 servings</u>

3 lbs. – pork chops

1 small onion sliced

1 small green bell pepper sliced

1 small red bell pepper sliced

1 tsp. season salt

1 tsp. black pepper

1 can of cream of mushroom

2 15oz cans of glory green beans - recipe on page 93

1 15oz can of cut spinach

8 potatoes – use forked potato recipe on page 91

1. Lightly brown meat in skillet then sprinkle seasoning salt and black pepper on meat first. Place browned meat in roast pan or 9x13 cake pan then pour 1 can of cream of mushroom sauce over meat.
2. Cover with lid or aluminum foil and bake 15 minutes.
3. Then uncover to add onions, green and red bell peppers. Cover and continue baking 15 minutes.
4. Stir gravy to make sure everything is thoroughly mixed.
5. 30 minutes before meat is done. Cook potatoes according to page 91 and make green beans page 93.

Put meat, green beans and potatoes on plates then pour gravy over potatoes and serve.

# "Fried Pork Steaks, Forked Potatoes and Corn on the Cob"

<u>Makes 8 servings</u>

3 lbs. – pork steaks

1 small onion sliced

1 small green bell pepper sliced

1 small red bell pepper sliced

1 tsp. season salt

1 tsp. black pepper

8 potatoes – use forked potato recipe on page 91

1. Place pork steaks in 9x13 cake pan then sprinkle seasoning salt and black pepper on meat first, also take a plastic bag and put flour in it. Use a double bag method, so flour won't spill out of the bag.
2. Toss individual pieces of meat in bag and shake until coated with flour. Pour vegetable oil in a skillet and heat oil until it pops a little. (Important) Place meat in hot skillet.
3. Cover and fry meat until golden brown on one side.
4. Then uncover and fry meat until golden brown on the other side. (Only cook 4 pieces at a time)
5. 30 minutes before meat is done. Cook potatoes according to page 91 and boil corn on the cob 10 minutes.

Put meat, potatoes and corn on the cob on plates then serve.

# "Fried Pork Steaks Smothered in gravy, Forked Potatoes and Biscuits"

<u>Makes 8 servings</u>

3 lbs. – pork steaks

1 small onion sliced

1 small green bell pepper sliced

1 small red bell pepper sliced

1 tsp. season salt and 1 tsp. black pepper

2 brown gravy packets with 2 cups of water

1 can of grand butter milk biscuits - recipe on page 104

8 potatoes – use forked potato recipe on page 91

1. Place pork steaks in 9x13 cake pan then sprinkle seasoning salt and black pepper on meat first, also take a plastic bag and put flour in it. Use a double bag method, so flour won't spill out of the bag.
2. Toss individual pieces of meat in bag and shake until coated with flour. Pour vegetable oil in a skillet and heat oil until it pops a little. (Important) Place meat in hot skillet.
3. Cover and fry meat until golden brown on one side.
4. Then uncover and fry meat until golden brown on the other side. (Only cook 4 pieces at a time) Drain grease from skillet then Place browned pork steaks and onions, green and red bell peppers in skillet then pour 2 cups of brown gravy mix over meat. Cover and cook 15 minutes.
5. 30 minutes before meat is done. Cook potatoes according to page 91 and make biscuits page 104 with butter.

Put meat and potatoes on plates with biscuits then pour gravy over potatoes and serve.

# "Baked Barbeque Pork Steaks, Forked Potatoes and Green Beans"

<u>Makes 8 servings</u>

3 lbs. – pork steaks

1 small onion sliced

1 small green bell pepper sliced

1 small red bell pepper sliced

1 tsp. season salt

1 tsp. black pepper

2 bottles of favorite barbeque sauce (Thick and spicy /the best)

2 15oz cans of glory green beans - recipe on page 93

8 potatoes – use forked potato recipe on page 91

1. Lightly brown pork steaks in skillet then sprinkle seasoning salt and black pepper on meat first. Place browned meat in roast pan or 9x13 cake pan then pour barbeque sauce over meat.
2. Cover with lid or aluminum foil and bake 15 minutes.
3. Then uncover to add more barbeque sauce, onions, green and red bell peppers and continue baking uncovered 15 minutes.
4. 30 minutes before meat is done. Cook potatoes according to page 91 and make green beans page 93.

Put meat, green beans and potatoes on plates then serve.

# "Fried Pork Rib-lets and Forked Potatoes"

<u>Makes 8 servings</u>

3 lbs. – pork rib-lets

1 small onion sliced

1 small green bell pepper sliced

1 small red bell pepper sliced

1 tsp. season salt

1 tsp. black pepper

8 potatoes – use forked potato recipe on page 91

1. Place pork rib-lets in 9x13 cake pan then sprinkle seasoning salt and black pepper on meat first, also take a plastic bag and put flour in it. Use a double bag method, so flour won't spill out of the bag.
2. Toss individual pieces of meat in bag and shake until coated with flour. Pour vegetable oil in a skillet and heat oil until it pops a little. (Important) Place meat in hot skillet.
3. Cover and fry meat until golden brown on one side.
4. Then uncover and fry meat until golden brown on the other side. (Only cook 4 pieces at a time)
5. 30 minutes before meat is done. Cook potatoes according to page 91.

Put meat and potatoes on plates then serve.

# "Fried Pork Rib-lets in Salsa over Rice"

<u>Makes 8 servings</u>

3 lbs. – cut up pork rib-lets

1 small onion sliced

1 small green bell pepper sliced

1 small red bell pepper sliced

1 tsp. season salt

1 tsp. black pepper

2 bottles of favorite salsa (Thick and chunky/the best)

Rice – use rice recipe on page 92 or Boil-a-bag rice in 10 minutes

1. Lightly brown pork rib-lets in skillet then sprinkle seasoning salt and black pepper on meat first. Place browned meat in roast pan or 9x13 cake pan then pour salsa over meat.
2. Cover with lid or aluminum foil and bake 15 minutes.
3. Then uncover to add more salsa, onions, green and red bell peppers and continue cooking uncovered 15 minutes.
4. 10 minutes before meal is done. Cook rice according to page 92.

Put rib-let sauce over rice on plates and serve.

# "Oven Pork Barbeque Ribs, Macaroni & Cheese and Greens"

<u>Makes 8 servings</u>

3 lbs. – pork ribs

1 small onion sliced

1 small green bell pepper sliced

1 small red bell pepper sliced

1 tsp. season salt

1 tsp. black pepper

2 bottles of favorite barbeque sauce (Thick and spicy /the best)

2 15oz cans of glory greens – recipe on page 95

Macaroni & cheese – use macaroni & cheese recipe on page 97

1. Cut meat slab in 1/3 then put in 5 quart pot and boil 30 minutes. Place pork ribs in roast pan or 9x13 cake pan then sprinkle seasoning salt and black pepper on meat first, also pour barbeque sauce over meat.
2. Cover with lid or aluminum foil and bake 15 minutes.
3. Then uncover to add more barbeque sauce, onions, green and red bell peppers and continue baking uncovered 15 minutes.
4. 30 minutes before meat is done. Cook macaroni & cheese according to page 97 and make greens page 95.

Put meat, greens and macaroni & cheese on plates then serve.

# "Oven Pork Country Barbeque Ribs, Macaroni & Cheese and Green Beans"

<u>Makes 8 servings</u>

3 lbs. – pork country ribs

1 small onion sliced

1 small green bell pepper sliced

1 small red bell pepper sliced

1 tsp. season salt

1 tsp. black pepper

2 bottles of favorite barbeque sauce (Thick and spicy /the best)

2 15oz cans of glory green beans - recipe on page 93

Macaroni & cheese – use macaroni & cheese recipe on page 97

1. Put country ribs in 5 quart pot and boil 30 minutes. Place country ribs in roast pan or 9x13 cake pan then sprinkle seasoning salt and black pepper on meat first, also pour barbeque sauce over meat.
2. Cover with lid or aluminum foil and bake 15 minutes.
3. Then uncover to add more barbeque sauce, onions, green and red bell peppers and continue baking uncovered 15 minutes.
4. 30 minutes before meat is done. Cook macaroni & cheese according to page 97 and make green beans page 93.

Put meat, green beans and macaroni & cheese on plates then serve.

# "Grilled Pork Ribs, Macaroni & Cheese and Green Beans"

<u>Makes 8 servings</u>

3 lbs. – pork ribs

1 small onion sliced

1 small green bell pepper sliced

1 small red bell pepper sliced

1 tsp. season salt

1 tsp. black pepper

2 bottles of favorite barbeque sauce (Thick and spicy /the best)

2 15oz cans of glory green beans – recipe on page 93

Macaroni & cheese – use macaroni & cheese recipe on page 97

1. Lightly brown pork ribs on grill then sprinkle seasoning salt and black pepper on meat first.
2. Place pork ribs in roast pan or 9x13 cake pan then pour barbeque sauce over meat.
3. Cover with lid or aluminum foil and bake 15 minutes.
4. Then uncover to add more barbeque sauce, onions, green and red bell peppers and continue cooking uncovered 15 minutes. (Also eat without sauce when grilled - no additional baking needed)
5. 30 minutes before meat is done. Cook macaroni & cheese according to page 97 and make green beans page 93.

Put meat, green beans and macaroni & cheese on plates then serve.

# "Smothered Potatoes and Polish Sausage"

<u>Makes 8 servings</u>

3 lbs. – polish sausage (Eckrich /the best)

1 small onion sliced

1 small green bell pepper sliced

1 small red bell pepper sliced

1 tsp. season salt

1 tsp. black pepper

8 potatoes

1. Peel 8 potatoes and slice like fries. Place raw sliced potatoes into a greased skillet then sprinkle seasoning salt and black pepper on potatoes first. Cook 10 minutes.
2. Cut polish sausage into circles and lightly brown in a different skillet. Place browned meat, onions, green and red bell peppers into the skillet with potatoes.
3. Cover and continue cooking 20 minutes turning potatoes periodically until tender and light brown.
4. 5 minutes before meal is done. (Important) Sprinkle a little water over potatoes and sausage mix for steam, moisture and tenderness.

Put smothered potatoes on plates and serve.

# "Smothered Cabbage and Polish Sausage"

<u>Makes 8 servings</u>

3 lbs. - polish sausage (Eckrich /the best)

1 small onion sliced

1 small green bell pepper sliced

1 small red bell pepper sliced

1 tsp. season salt

1 tsp. black pepper

1 cabbage

1. Chop cabbage and place into a greased skillet then sprinkle seasoning salt and black pepper on cabbage first. Cook 10 minutes.
2. Cut polish sausage into circles and lightly brown in a different skillet. Place browned meat, onions, green and red bell peppers into the skillet with cabbage.
3. Cover and continue cooking 20 minutes turning cabbage periodically until tender.

Put smothered cabbage on plates and serve.

# "Fried Polish Sausage Sandwich and Fries"

<u>Makes 8 servings</u>

3 lbs. - polish sausage (Eckrich /the best)

1 small onion sliced

1 small green bell pepper sliced

1 small red bell pepper sliced

1 tsp. season salt

1 tsp. black pepper

1. Cut polish sausage into hot dog size pieces, slice down the middle to open and lightly brown in a skillet.
2. Place polish sausage on buns.
3. Sautee season salt, black pepper, onions, green and red bell peppers to put on your plate. (If you desire the flavor)
4. Start cooking fries according to package first before meat.

Put sandwiches and fries on plates then serve.

# "Fried Brat Sandwich and Forked Potatoes"

<u>Makes 8 servings</u>

3 lbs. – brats (Johnsonville /the best)

1 small onion sliced

1 small green bell pepper sliced

1 small red bell pepper sliced

1 tsp. season salt

1 tsp. black pepper

8 potatoes – use forked potato recipe on page 91

1.  Boil brats in 5 quart pan 10 minutes.
2.  Place brats into a skillet, cover and lightly brown on both sides 10 minutes.
3.  Then uncover poke brats with a knife to release juices, add season salt, black pepper, onions, green and red bell peppers and continue cooking covered 5 minutes.
4.  Place brats into buns with onions and peppers.
5.  30 minutes before meat is done. Cook potatoes according to page 91.

Put sandwiches and potatoes on plates then serve.

# "Grilled Brats and Macaroni & Cheese"

<u>Makes 8 servings</u>

3 lbs. - brats (Johnsonville /the best)

1 small onion sliced

1 small green bell pepper sliced

1 small red bell pepper sliced

1 tsp. season salt

1 tsp. black pepper

Macaroni & cheese – use macaroni & cheese recipe on page 97

1. Lightly brown brats on grill.
2. Place brats into a skillet with season salt, black pepper, onions, green and red bell peppers and continue cooking covered 5 minutes.
3. Place brats into buns with onions and peppers.
4. 10 minutes before meat is done. Cook macaroni & cheese according to page 97.

Put sandwiches and macaroni & cheese on plates then serve.

# "Baked Ham, Macaroni & Cheese and Greens"

<u>Makes 8 servings</u>

12 lbs. - ham

1 small onion sliced

1 small green bell pepper sliced

1 small red bell pepper sliced

1 tsp. season salt

1 tsp. black pepper

2 15oz cans of glory greens – recipe on page 95

Macaroni & cheese – use macaroni & cheese recipe on page 97

1. Place ham in roast pan or 9x13 cake pan.
2. Cover with lid or aluminum foil and bake 2 hours.
3. Sautee season salt, black pepper, onions, green and red bell peppers to put on your plate. (If you desire the flavor)
4. 30 minutes before meat is done. Cook macaroni & cheese according to page 97 and make greens page 95.

Put meat, greens and macaroni & cheese on plates then serve.

# *"Fried Ham Sandwich and Chips"*

<u>Makes 8 servings</u>

1 lb. – ham

1 small onion sliced

1 small green bell pepper sliced

1 small red bell pepper sliced

1 tsp. season salt

1 tsp. black pepper

1 loaf of bread

1 bag of your favorite chips

1. Lightly brown ham in a skillet. (Slices from a previously cook ham are best)
2. Place ham on buns with mayonnaise.
3. Sautee season salt, black pepper, onions, green and red bell peppers to put on your plate. (If you desire the flavor)
4. After meat is done. Select your favorite chips.

Put sandwiches and chips on plates then serve.

# "Fried Ham, Cheesy Eggs and Toast"

Makes 8 servings

1 lb. – ham

1 dozen eggs

1 small onion sliced

1 small green bell pepper sliced

1 small red bell pepper sliced

1 tsp. season salt

1 tsp. black pepper

1 loaf of bread

1. Lightly brown ham in a skillet. (Slices from a previously cook ham are best)
2. Cook eggs in a separate skillet with season salt, black pepper, onions, green and red bell peppers and blended cheeses.
3. Then make toast.

Put ham, eggs and toast on plates then serve.

# *"Fried Diced Ham in Cheesy Eggs, O'Brien Potatoes and Toast"*

<u>Makes 8 servings</u>

1 lb. – diced ham

1 dozen eggs

1 small onion sliced

1 small green bell pepper sliced

1 small red bell pepper sliced

1 tsp. season salt

1 tsp. black pepper

1 loaf of bread

1 bag of O'brien potatoes

1. Lightly brown diced ham in a skillet. (Slices diced from a previously cook ham are best)
2. Cook eggs in a separate skillet with browned diced ham, season salt, black pepper, onions, green and red bell peppers and blended cheeses.
3. Cook Obrien potatoes in a separate greased skillet turning until light brown and tender.
4. Then make toast.

Put cheesy eggs, potatoes and toast on plates then serve.

# "Fried Sausage, Ham, Bacon, Cheesy Eggs and Toast"

<u>Makes 8 servings</u>

1 lb. sausage, 1 lb. ham and 1 lb. bacon

1 dozen eggs

1 small onion sliced

1 small green bell pepper sliced

1 small red bell pepper sliced

1 tsp. season salt

1 tsp. black pepper

1 loaf of bread

1. Lightly brown meats in separate skillets first.
2. Cook eggs in a separate skillet with season salt, black pepper, onions, green and red bell peppers and blended cheeses.
3. Then make toast.

Put meats, eggs and toast on plates then serve.

# *"Fried Crumbled Sausage in Rice"*

<u>Makes 8 servings</u>

3 lbs. – sausage (Jimmy deans sage / the best)

1 small onion sliced

1 small green bell pepper sliced

1 small red bell pepper sliced

1 tsp. season salt

1 tsp. black pepper

2 small boxes of Dirty Rice

5 cups of water

1. Lightly brown meat in skillet then sprinkle seasoning salt and black pepper on meat first, also add onions, green and red bell peppers.
2. Place browned meat mixture and dirty rice mix in 5 quart pot with 5 cups of water then stir.
3. Cover and cook on low 25 minutes.
4. Stir to make sure everything is thoroughly mixed.

Put sausage rice in bowls and serve.

# "Fried Crumbled Italian Sausage and Rice in Stuffed Peppers"

<u>Makes 8 servings</u>

3 lbs. – Italian sausage (Jimmy deans / the best)

1 small onion sliced

7 small green bell pepper sliced

1 small red bell pepper sliced

1 tsp. season salt

1 tsp. black pepper

2 small boxes of Dirty Rice

5 cups of water

1. Lightly brown meat in skillet then sprinkle seasoning salt and black pepper on meat first, also add onions, green and red bell peppers.
2. Place browned meat mixture and dirty rice mix in 5 quart pot with 5 cups of water then stir.
3. Cover and cook on low 25 minutes.
4. Stir to make sure everything is thoroughly mixed.
5. Carve out the inside of green peppers and fill with meat mixture. Place in 9x13 cake pan and bake 25 minutes.

Put stuffed peppers on plates and serve.

# *"Ham and Great Northern Beans"*

<u>Makes 8 servings</u>

1 lb. - Ham

1 small onion sliced

1 small green bell pepper sliced

1 small red bell pepper sliced

1 tsp. season salt

1 tsp. black pepper

2 lbs. package of great northern beans

6 cups of water

1. Rinse beans, before putting into a 5 quart pot with 6 cups of water then sprinkle seasoning salt, black pepper and 1 Tsp. of vegetables oil on them first.
2. Cover and cook 2 hours.
3. Lightly brown ham in skillet.
4. Then uncover beans to add browned meat, onions, green and red bell peppers. Cover and continue cooking 1 hour.
5. Stir to make sure everything is thoroughly mixed.

Put beans in bowl and serve with crackers or cornbread.

# "Ham and Pinto Beans"

<u>Makes 8 servings</u>

1 lb. - Ham

1 small onion sliced

1 small green bell pepper sliced

1 small red bell pepper sliced

1 tsp. season salt

1 tsp. black pepper

2 lbs. package of pinto beans

6 cups of water

1. Rinse beans, before putting into a 5 quart pot with 6 cups of water then sprinkle seasoning salt, black pepper and 1 Tsp. of vegetables oil on them first.
2. Cover and cook 2 hours.
3. Lightly brown ham in skillet.
4. Then uncover beans to add browned meat, onions, green and red bell peppers. Cover and continue cooking 1 hour.
5. Stir to make sure everything is thoroughly mixed.

Put beans in bowl and serve with crackers or cornbread.

# "Bacon and Pinto Beans"

<u>Makes 8 servings</u>

1 lb. - bacon

1 small onion sliced

1 small green bell pepper sliced

1 small red bell pepper sliced

1 tsp. season salt

1 tsp. black pepper

2 lbs. package of pinto beans

6 cups of water

1. Rinse beans, before putting into a 5 quart pot with 6 cups of water then sprinkle seasoning salt, black pepper and 1 Tsp. of vegetables oil on them first.
2. Cover and cook 2 hours.
3. Lightly brown bacon in skillet.
4. Then uncover beans to add browned meat, onions, green and red bell peppers. Cover and continue cooking 1 hour.
5. Stir to make sure everything is thoroughly mixed.

Put beans in bowl and serve with crackers or cornbread.

# "Tender Neck-bones and Forked Potatoes"

<u>Makes 8 servings</u>

3 lbs. – neck-bones

1 small onion sliced

1 small green bell pepper sliced

1 small red bell pepper sliced

1 tsp. season salt

1 tsp. black pepper

1 beef stew seasoning packet with 1 cup of water

8 potatoes – use forked potato recipe on page 91

6 cups of water

1. Boil neck-bones in a 5 quart pot with 6 cups of water then sprinkle seasoning salt, black pepper, beef stew seasoning and 1 Tsp. of vegetables oil on them first.
2. Cover and cook 2 hours.
3. 30 minutes before meat is done. Cook potatoes according to page 91.

Put meat and potatoes on plates then serve.

# "Fried Catfish and Spaghetti"

Makes 8 servings

3 lbs. – catfish

1 small onion sliced

1 small green bell pepper sliced

1 small red bell pepper sliced

1 tsp. season salt

1 tsp. black pepper

1 jar of favorite spaghetti sauce

1 can of tomato juice

1 package of spaghetti – use spaghetti recipe on page 28

1. Place catfish in 9x13 cake pan then sprinkle seasoning salt and black pepper on fish first, also take a plastic bag and put corn meal in it. Use a double bag method, so corn meal won't spill out of the bag.
2. Toss individual pieces of fish in bag and shake until coated with corn meal. Pour vegetable oil in a skillet and heat oil until it pops a little. (Important) Place fish in hot skillet.
3. Cover and fry fish until golden brown on one side.
4. Then uncover and fry fish until golden brown on the other side. (Only cook 4 pieces at a time)
5. 30 minutes before fish is done. Cook spaghetti according to page 28. (Elbow noodles are best)

Put fish and spaghetti on plates then serve.

# "Fried Perch Fish and Spaghetti"

<u>Makes 8 servings</u>

3 lbs. – perch fish

1 small onion sliced

1 small green bell pepper sliced

1 small red bell pepper sliced

1 tsp. season salt

1 tsp. black pepper

1 jar of favorite spaghetti sauce

1 can of tomato juice

1 package of spaghetti – use spaghetti recipe on page 28

1. Place perch fish in 9x13 cake pan then sprinkle seasoning salt and black pepper on fish first, also take a plastic bag and put corn meal in it. Use a double bag method, so corn meal won't spill out of the bag.
2. Toss individual pieces of fish in bag and shake until coated with corn meal. Pour vegetable oil in a skillet and heat oil until it pops a little. (Important) Place fish in hot skillet.
3. Cover and fry fish until golden brown on one side.
4. Then uncover and fry fish until golden brown on the other side. (Only cook 4 pieces at a time)
5. 30 minutes before fish is done. Cook spaghetti according to page 28. (Elbow noodles are best)

Put fish and spaghetti on plates then serve.

# "Fried Tilapia Fish and Spaghetti"

<u>Makes 8 servings</u>

3 lbs. – tilapia fish

1 small onion sliced

1 small green bell pepper sliced

1 small red bell pepper sliced

1 tsp. season salt

1 tsp. black pepper

1 jar of favorite spaghetti sauce

1 can of tomato juice

1 package of spaghetti – use spaghetti recipe on page 28

1. Place tilapia fish in 9x13 cake pan then sprinkle seasoning salt and black pepper on fish first, also take a plastic bag and put corn meal in it. Use a double bag method, so corn meal won't spill out of the bag.
2. Toss individual pieces of fish in bag and shake until coated with corn meal. Pour vegetable oil in a skillet and heat oil until it pops a little. (Important) Place fish in hot skillet.
3. Cover and fry fish until golden brown on one side.
4. Then uncover and fry fish until golden brown on the other side. (Only cook 4 pieces at a time)
5. 30 minutes before fish is done. Cook spaghetti according to page 28. (Elbow noodles are best)

Put fish and spaghetti on plates then serve.

# *"Fried Catfish Nuggets and Fries"*

<u>Makes 8 servings</u>

3 lbs. – catfish or catfish nuggets

1 small onion sliced

1 small green bell pepper sliced

1 small red bell pepper sliced

1 tsp. season salt

1 tsp. black pepper

1 bag of your favorite fries

1.  Place cut up catfish in 9x13 cake pan then sprinkle seasoning salt and black pepper on fish first, also take a plastic bag and put corn meal in it. Use a double bag method, so corn meal won't spill out of the bag.
2.  Toss individual pieces of fish in bag and shake until coated with corn meal. Pour vegetable oil in a skillet and heat oil until it pops a little. (Important) Place fish in hot skillet.
3.  Cover and fry fish until golden brown on one side.
4.  Then uncover and fry fish until golden brown on the other side. (Only cook 8 pieces at a time)
5.  Sautee season salt, black pepper, onions, green and red bell peppers to put on your plate. (If you desire the flavor)
6.  30 minutes before fish is done. Cook fries according to package.

Put fish and fries on plates then serve.

# "Fried Shrimp and Fries"

<u>Makes 8 servings</u>

3 lbs. – jumbo shrimp

1 small onion sliced

1 small green bell pepper sliced

1 small red bell pepper sliced

1 tsp. season salt

1 tsp. black pepper

1 bag of your favorite fries

1. Place shrimp in 9x13 cake pan then sprinkle seasoning salt and black pepper on shrimp first, also take a plastic bag and put corn meal in it. Use a double bag method, so corn meal won't spill out of the bag.
2. Toss individual pieces of shrimp in bag and shake until coated with corn meal. Pour vegetable oil in a skillet and heat oil until it pops a little. (Important) Place shrimp in hot skillet.
3. Fry shrimp until golden brown on both sides.
4. Sautee season salt, black pepper, onions, green and red bell peppers to put on your plate. (If you desire the flavor)
5. 30 minutes before shrimp is done. Cook fries according to package.

Put shrimp and fries on plates then serve.

# "Sautéed Shrimp over Broccoli and Cheddar Rice"

<u>Makes 8 servings</u>

3 lbs. – jumbo shrimp

1 small onion sliced

1 small green bell pepper sliced

1 small red bell pepper sliced

1 tsp. season salt

1 tsp. black pepper

2 broccoli and cheddar rice packages with 2 cups of water

1. Place shrimp in 9x13 cake pan then sprinkle seasoning salt and black pepper on shrimp first.
2. Sautee shrimp in butter with onions, green and red bell peppers until golden brown on both sides.
3. 30 minutes before shrimp is done. Cook broccoli cheddar rice according to package.

Put shrimp and rice on plates then serve.

# "Sautéed Tilapia over Broccoli and Cheddar Rice"

<u>Makes 8 servings</u>

3 lbs. – tilapia

1 small onion sliced

1 small green bell pepper sliced

1 small red bell pepper sliced

1 tsp. season salt

1 tsp. black pepper

2 broccoli and cheddar rice packages with 2 cups of water

1. Place tilapia in 9x13 cake pan then sprinkle seasoning salt and black pepper on fish first.
2. Sautee fish in butter with onions, green and red bell peppers until golden brown on both sides.
3. 30 minutes before fish is done. Cook broccoli cheddar rice according to package.

Put fish and rice on plates then serve.

# "Roasted Turkey, Macaroni & Cheese and Green Beans"

<u>Makes 8 servings</u>

12 lbs. – turkey

1 small onion sliced

1 small green bell pepper sliced

1 small red bell pepper sliced

1 tsp. season salt

1 tsp. black pepper

2 15oz cans of glory green beans – recipe on page 93

Macaroni & cheese – use macaroni & cheese recipe on page 97

1. First rub vegetable oil all over turkey then sprinkle seasoning salt and black pepper on meat first.
2. Place turkey in roast pan or 9x13 cake pan.
3. Cover with lid or aluminum foil and bake 2 hours.
4. Sautee season salt, black pepper, onions, green and red bell peppers to put on your plate. (If you desire the flavor)
5. 30 minutes before meat is done. Cook macaroni & cheese according to page 97 and make green beans page 93.

Put meat, green beans and macaroni & cheese on plates then serve.

# "Awesome Turkey Hash Left-Over with Potatoes and Biscuits"

<u>Makes 8 servings</u>

3 lbs. - turkey

1 small onion sliced

1 small green bell pepper sliced

1 small red bell pepper sliced

1 tsp. season salt

1 tsp. black pepper

1 beef stew seasoning packet with 1 cup of water

1 can of grand butter milk biscuits - recipe on page 104

8 potatoes

1. Peel 8 potatoes and dice them. Place diced potatoes into a greased skillet then sprinkle seasoning salt and black pepper on potatoes first. Cook 10 minutes.
2. Shred meat from previously cook turkey. Place meat, onions, green and red bell peppers into the skillet with potatoes.
3. Cover and continue cooking 30 minutes turning potatoes periodically until tender and light brown gravy appears.
4. Stir to make sure everything is thoroughly mixed.
5. 30 minutes before meal is done. Cook biscuits according to page 104 with butter.

Put meat and potatoes on plates with biscuits then serve.

# "Turkey, Ham and Bacon Sandwich with Chips"

<u>Makes 8 servings</u>

1 lb. turkey, 1 lb. ham and 1 lb. bacon (Deli or package meats)

1 small onion sliced

1 small green bell pepper sliced

1 small red bell pepper sliced

1 tsp. season salt

1 tsp. black pepper

1 bag of your favorite chips

1. Lightly brown bacon in skillet
2. Place turkey, ham and bacon on buns with mayonnaise, mustard, onions, tomatoes and lettuce.
3. Sautee season salt, black pepper, onions, green and red bell peppers to put on your plate. (If you desire the flavor)

Put sandwiches and favorite chips on plates then serve.

# "Forked Potatoes"

1 tsp. salt

1 tsp. black pepper

1 stick of butter

8 potatoes

1. Peel 8 potatoes and cut them into 4 pieces each.
2. Boil potatoes into a 5 quart pot with 6 cups of water.
3. Cover and cook 30 minutes.
4. When potatoes are tender add butter, salt and black pepper.
5. Fork to make sure everything is thoroughly mixed.

Put potatoes on plates and serve.

# *"Rice"*

<u>Makes 8 servings</u>

1 tsp. salt

1 tsp. black pepper

1 stick of butter

Rice – use Boil-a-bag rice in 10 minutes

1. Boil 4 rice bags into 5 quart pot with 6 cups of water.
2. Cover and cook 15minutes.
3. When rice is done.
4. Cut open pouches and put rice in large bowl with butter, salt and black pepper.
5. Stir to make sure everything is thoroughly mixed.

Put rice on plates and serve.

# "Green Beans and Bacon"

<u>Makes 8 servings</u>

1 small onion sliced

1 small green bell pepper sliced

1 small red bell pepper sliced

1 tsp. season salt

1 tsp. black pepper

2 15oz can of glory green beans

1. Lightly brown bacon in skillet.
2. Boil green beans in 5 quart pot with bacon, season salt, black pepper, onions, green and red bell peppers.
3. Cover and cook 15minutes.
4. Stir to make sure everything is thoroughly mixed.

Put green beans on plates and serve.

# "Greens and Bacon from Bunch Stalks"

<u>Makes 8 servings</u>

1 lb. bacon

1 small onion sliced

1 tsp. season salt

1 tsp. black pepper

1 bunch stalk of mustard greens

1 bunch stalk of turnip greens

1 15oz can of spinach

1. Lightly brown bacon in skillet.
2. Boil greens, spinach and bacon in 5 quart pot with a 1 Tsp. of vegetable oil, season salt, black pepper, and onions.
3. Cover and cook 30minutes.
4. Uncover chop greens with knife periodically for tenderness. Cover and continue cooking 30 minutes until tender.
5. Stir to make sure everything is thoroughly mixed.

Put greens on plates and serve.

# "Easy Greens and Bacon / Canned"

<u>Makes 8 servings</u>

1 lb. bacon

1 small onion sliced

1 tsp. season salt

1 tsp. black pepper

1 15oz can of spinach

2 15oz can of glory green beans

1. Lightly brown bacon in skillet.
2. Boil greens, spinach and bacon in 5 quart pot with season salt, black pepper and onions.
3. Cover and cook 15minutes.
4. Stir to make sure everything is thoroughly mixed.

Put greens on plates and serve.

# *"Baked Macaroni & Cheese"*

<u>Makes 8 servings</u>

1 tsp. season salt

1 tsp. black pepper

2 bags of blended cheese and 1 cup of milk

1 box of Elbow noodles and 1 egg

1. Boil macaroni in 5 quart pot with 6 cups of water.
2. Cover and cook 15minutes.
3. Uncover and pour macaroni into glass baking pan with cheese, egg, milk, season salt and black pepper.
4. Stir to make sure everything is thoroughly mixed.
5. Bake 30 minutes.

Put macaroni and cheese on plates and serve.

# *"Easy Macaroni & Cheese / Box"*

<u>Makes 8 servings</u>

1 tsp. salt

1 tsp. black pepper

2 bags of blended cheeses

2 boxes of macaroni and cheese

1. Boil macaroni in 5 quart pot with 6 cups of water.
2. Cover and cook 15minutes.
3. Uncover and add blended cheeses, season salt and black pepper.
4. Cover and continue cooking 5 minutes until tender and creamy.
5. Stir to make sure everything is thoroughly mixed.

Put macaroni and cheese on plates and serve.

# *"Beef Rice / Box"*

<u>Makes 8 servings</u>

2 small boxes of beef Rice a Roni

5 cups of water

1.  Lightly brown rice & vermicelli with butter in skillet. Place beef seasoning, onions, green and red bell peppers, rice and vermicelli in 5 quart pot with 5 cups of water then stir.
2.  Cover and cook on low 30 minutes.
3.  Stir to make sure everything is thoroughly mixed.

Put rice in bowls and serve.

# *"Chicken Rice / Box"*

<u>Makes 8 servings</u>

2 small boxes of chicken Rice a Roni

5 cups of water

1. Lightly brown rice & vermicelli with butter in skillet. Place chicken seasoning, onions, green and red bell peppers, rice and vermicelli in 5 quart pot with 5 cups of water then stir.
2. Cover and cook on low 30 minutes.
3. Stir to make sure everything is thoroughly mixed.

Put rice in bowls and serve.

# "Instant Baby Red Potatoes"

<u>Makes 8 servings</u>

1 tsp. salt

1 tsp. black pepper

1 stick of butter

2 baby reds instant potato packages with 2 cups of water

1. Boil 2 cups of water 10 minutes.
2. Remove from heat and add instant potatoes with butter, salt and black pepper.
3. Stir to make sure everything is thoroughly mixed.

Put potatoes on plates and serve.

# *"Red Potatoes for Boiled Stews"*

<u>Makes 8 servings</u>

1 tsp. salt

1 tsp. black pepper

1 stick of butter

8 red potatoes

1. Peel 8 potatoes and cut them into 4 pieces each.
2. Boil potatoes into a 5 quart pot with 6 cups of water.
3. Cover and cook 30 minutes.
4. When potatoes are tender add butter, salt and black pepper. (Also put in stews)

Put potatoes on plates and serve.

# *"Cheesy Red Potatoes and Bacon"*

<u>Makes 8 servings</u>

1lb. bacon

1 tsp. salt

1 tsp. black pepper

1 bag of blended cheeses

1 jar of mayonnaise

1 tub of sour cream

1 stick of butter

8 red potatoes

1. Peel 8 potatoes and cut them into 4 pieces each.
2. Boil potatoes into a 5 quart pot with 6 cups of water.
3. Cover and cook 15 minutes.
4. Lightly brown bacon in skillet.
5. Place potatoes and crumbled bacon in 9x13 cake pan with butter, mayonnaise, sour cream and blended cheeses.
6. Cover with lid or aluminum foil and bake 25 minutes.

Put potatoes on plates and serve.

# "Chili Cheese Baked Potatoes"

1 - 8oz. bag of blended cheese

Chili – use chili recipe page 29

8 potatoes

1. Poke potatoes all over with knife then wrap in aluminum foil.
2. Place wrapped potatoes in 9x13 cake pan and bake 2 hours.
3. Un-wrap potatoes and slice down the middle to open.
4. Pour chili over potatoes from awesome chili recipe page 29 then sprinkle cheese over chili.

Put chili cheese bake potatoes on plates and serve.

# *"Easy Biscuits / Can"*

<u>Makes 8 servings</u>

1 can of grand butter milk biscuits

1. Place biscuits on pan and put in the over.
2. Bake 20 minutes.
3. Remove from oven and butter top of biscuits.

Put biscuits on plates and serve.

# "Butter Pecan Bundt Cake with Sugar Glaze Frosting"

<u>Makes 8 servings</u>

1 box of butter pecan cake mix

1 bag of powdered sugar

3 eggs

1 Tsp. of vegetable oil

1 cup of water

1.  Put 1 Tsp. of vegetable oil in bundt pan and place in oven 5 minutes then spread oil evenly around pan and flour.
2.  Put cake mix into a bowl and add in a few drops of oil that was previously heated, eggs and water.
3.  Stir to make sure everything is thoroughly mixed.
4.  Pour cake batter into round bundt cake pan then place in oven.
5.  Bake 35 minutes.
6.  Remove from oven and let cool 5 minutes then flip over on plate.
7.  Stir powdered sugar with water then pour over cake.

Put cake on plates and serve.

# "White Cake & Strawberry Filling with Whip Cream Frosting"

<u>Makes 8 servings</u>

1 box of white cake mix

1 bottle of strawberry syrup – (Hershey's/the best)

1 can of whip cream frosting

3 eggs

1 Tsp. of vegetable oil

1 cup of water

1. Put 1 Tsp. of vegetable oil in 9x13 pan and place in oven 5 minutes then spread oil evenly around pan and flour.
2. Put cake mix into a bowl and add in a few drops of oil that was previously heated, eggs and water.
3. Stir to make sure everything is thoroughly mixed.
4. Pour cake batter into 9x13 cake pan then place in oven.
5. Bake 35 minutes.
6. Remove from oven and let cool 5 minutes then poke holes all over cake.
7. Pour strawberry syrup into holes then frost cake with whip cream frosting.

Put cake on plates and serve.

# "Marble Cake with Milk Chocolate Frosting"

<u>Makes 8 servings</u>

1 box of marble cake mix

1 can of milk chocolate frosting

3 eggs

1 Tsp. of vegetable oil

1 cup of water

1. Put 1 Tsp. of vegetable oil in 9x13 pan and place in oven 5 minutes then spread oil evenly around pan and flour.
2. Put cake mix into a bowl and add in a few drops of oil that was previously heated, eggs and water.
3. Also take a little batter and stir with coco mix.
4. Stir to make sure everything is thoroughly mixed.
5. Pour cake batter into 9x13 cake pan and swirl in coco mix then place in oven.
6. Bake 35 minutes.
7. Remove from oven and let cool 5 minutes then frost cake with milk chocolate frosting.

Put cake on plates and serve.

# "Chocolate Cake & Walnuts with Chocolate Frosting"

<u>Makes 8 servings</u>

1 box of chocolate cake mix

1 can of chocolate frosting

1 bag of walnuts

3 eggs

1 Tsp. of vegetable oil

1 cup of water

1. Put 1 Tsp. of vegetable oil in 9x13 pan and place in oven 5 minutes then spread oil evenly around pan and flour.
2. Put cake mix into a bowl and add in a few drops of oil that was previously heated, eggs and water then sprinkle in crushed walnuts.
3. Stir to make sure everything is thoroughly mixed.
4. Pour cake batter into 9x13 cake pan then place in oven.
5. Bake 35 minutes.
6. Remove from oven and let cool 5 minutes then frost cake with chocolate frosting.

Put cake on plates and serve.

# "Brownie Squares & Walnuts with Chocolate Frosting"

<u>Makes 8 servings</u>

1 box of brownie mix

1 can of chocolate frosting

1 bag of walnuts

2 eggs

1 Tsp. of vegetable oil

1 cup of water

1. Put 1 Tsp. of vegetable oil in 9x13 pan and place in oven 5 minutes then spread oil evenly around pan.
2. Put brownie mix into a bowl and add in a few drops of oil that was previously heated, egg and water then sprinkle in crushed walnuts.
3. Stir to make sure everything is thoroughly mixed.
4. Pour brownie mix into 9x13 cake pan then place in oven.
5. Bake 35 minutes.
6. Remove from oven and let cool 5 minutes then frost brownies with chocolate frosting.

Put cake on plates and serve.

# *"Sweet Potato Pie"*

<u>Makes 8 servings</u>

1 stick of butter

3 eggs

1 bottle of vanilla extract

1 bag of sugar

1 bag of brown sugar

8 sweet potatoes

1. Peel 8 potatoes and cut them in half.
2. Boil potatoes into a 5 quart pot with 6 cups of water.
3. Cover and cook 30 minutes.
4. When potatoes are tender, drain water and add eggs, butter, vanilla, sugar and brown sugar.
5. Stir to make sure everything is thoroughly mixed.
6. Pour sweet potato mix into round pie pan with crust.
7. Wrap edges of crust with aluminum foil, but not the center of pie then place in the oven.
8. Bake 1 hour.
9. Remove from oven and let cool 5 minutes.

Put sweet potato pie on plates and serve.

# "Chili Cheese Dip"

<u>Makes 8 servings</u>

1lb. hamburger

1lb. – block of spicy mexican process cheese spread

Chili – use chili recipe page 29 or can of Hormel chili with beans

1. Lightly brown meat in skillet then sprinkle seasoning salt and black pepper on meat first. Drain grease.
2. Combine hamburger, chili, and cheese in crock-pot.
3. Cover and cook on low 2 hours.
4. Stir periodically to make sure everything is thoroughly mixed.
5. Note: you do not half to use hamburger, if you made chili from page 29 recently. (Use that chili)

Put chili cheese dip with tortilla chips on plates and serve.

# *"Queso Cheese Dip"*

1lb. pork sausage (Jimmy deans sage /the best)

I - 8oz. can of diced tomatoes

½ cup of milk

1lb. – block of spicy mexican process cheese spread

1. Lightly brown meat in skillet then sprinkle seasoning salt and black pepper on meat first. Drain grease.
2. Combine sausage, diced tomatoes, milk and cheese in crock-pot.
3. Cover and cook on low 2 hours.
4. Stir periodically to make sure everything is thoroughly mixed.

Put queso cheese dip with tortilla chips on plates and serve.

# *"CONCLUSION"*

Please don't waste your time cooking food that people won't eat.

Only cook good tasting food that people will eat and enjoy.

This book will help you do that. People love eating my food.

This is my secret to successful cooking.

By Chef John Dye

# "DID THIS BOOK HELP YOU"

If so please send your replies & testimonies to the address below.

Chef: John Dye is available for Catered Events, Parties, Private dining and Speaking.

# "THANKS FOR YOUR SUPPORT"

I want to thank you for supporting me.

I really appreciate you helping me get the *"Word"* out about my New Cook Book.

I want you to know your contribution has not been in vain, but it has gone toward making the world better. Your gift is part of that effort and letting people know is the other part.

Thank you, once again for your support.

# "CONTRIBUTIONS"

**If you wish to send future contributions / send support to:**

Attn: Chef John Dye
P.O. Box 722
Mishawaka, Indiana 46546
Cell: (574) 220-3363
Email: johndyecookbook@yahoo.com

Sincerely,

Chef John Dye

# *"Index"*

## Appetizers:

1. Chili Cheese Dip
2. Queso Cheese Dip

## Breakfast:

1. Fried Ham Sandwich and Chips
2. Fried Ham, Cheesy Eggs and Toast
3. Diced Fried Ham in Cheesy Eggs, O'Brien Potatoes and Toast
4. Fried Sausage, Ham, Bacon, Cheesy Eggs and Toast

## Desserts:

1. Butter Pecan Bundt Cake with Sugar Glaze Frosting
2. White Cake & Strawberry Filling with Whip Cream Frosting
3. Marble Cake with Milk Chocolate Frosting
4. Chocolate Cake & Walnuts with Chocolate Frosting
5. Brownie Squares & Walnuts with Chocolate Frosting
6. Sweet Potato Pie

# "Index / Meats"

**Beef:**

# "Index / Meats"

**Chicken:**

1. Jambalaya with Chicken, Ham and Polish Sausage
2. Grilled Chicken Breast, Forked Potatoes and Green Beans
3. Baked Chicken Breast, Forked Potatoes and Greens
4. Baked Barbeque Chicken, Forked Potatoes and Green Beans
5. Chicken and Dressing
6. Roasted Chicken, Corn and Greens
7. Chicken Chunks and Broccoli Cheddar Rice Casserole
8. Cheesy Chicken Enchiladas
9. Fried Chicken and Smothered Potatoes
10. Fried Chicken Wing Sections Tossed in Favorite Hot Sauce
11. Fried Chicken Wing Sections Tossed in Favorite Barbeque Sauce
12. Fried Chicken Wing Sections Tossed in Jamaican Jerk Sauce
13. Fried Chicken Strips and Fries
14. Fried Chicken Breast Sandwich and Fries
15. Grilled Chicken Breast Sandwich and fries
16. Chicken Fajitas
17. Chicken, Beef and Polish Sausage Boil
18. Whole Fried Chicken Wings and Spaghetti
19. Chicken Stew Sauce over Rice

# "Index / Meats"

**Pork:**

1. Pork Stew Sauce over Rice
2. Pulled Pork Sandwich and Chips
3. Fried Pork Chops and Spaghetti
4. Fried Pork Chops, Smothered Potatoes and Corn on the Cob
5. Fried Pork Chops Smothered in Gravy, Forked Potatoes and Biscuits
6. Fried Pork Chop Sandwich and Forked Potatoes
7. Baked Pork Chops, Forked Potatoes and Green Beans
8. Fried Pork Steak, Forked Potatoes and Corn on the Cob
9. Fried Pork Steaks Smothered in Gravy, Forked Potatoes and Biscuits
10. Baked Barbeque Pork Steak, Forked Potatoes and Green Beans
11. Fried Pork Rib-lets and Forked Potatoes
12. Fried Pork Rib-lets in Salsa over Rice
13. Oven Pork Barbeque Ribs, Macaroni & Cheese and Greens
14. Oven Country Barbeque Ribs, Macaroni & Cheese and Green Beans
15. Grilled Pork Ribs, Macaroni & Cheese and Green Beans
16. Smothered Potatoes and Polish Sausage
17. Smothered Cabbage and Polish Sausage
18. Fried Polish Sausage Sandwich and Fries
19. Fried Brat Sandwich and Forked Potatoes
20. Grilled Brats and Macaroni & Cheese
21. Baked Ham, Macaroni & Cheese and Greens
22. Fried Ham Sandwich and Chips
23. Fried Ham, Cheesy Eggs and Toast

# *"Index / Meats"*

**Pork:**

# *"Index / Meats"*

**Seafood:**

1. Fried Catfish and Spaghetti
2. Fried Perch Fish and Spaghetti
3. Fried Tilapia Fish and Spaghetti
4. Fried Catfish Nuggets and Fries
5. Fried Shrimp and Fries
6. Sautéed Shrimp over Broccoli Cheddar Rice
7. Sautéed Tilapia over Broccoli Cheddar Rice

**Turkey:**

1. Roasted Turkey, Macaroni & Cheese and Green Beans
2. Awesome Turkey Hash with Potatoes Left-Over and Biscuits

# *"Index"*

## Sandwiches:

## Sides:

# *"Index"*

**Soup and Stews:**

# *"About The Author"*

**Biography:**

John Dye is an Author, Model, Actor, Motivational Speaker, Spiritual Counselor and Chef that has been cooking for many years and has decided to share his good tasting recipes with the world. This book is written to provide good tasting food to people, who love to eat with easy to use recipes.

Printed in the United States
By Bookmasters